WHAT ON EARTH?

WIND

Explore, create, and investigate!

Isabel Thomas
Pau Morgan

Contents

Wind and Weather

The Power of Wind

Read the legend of the Wind Eagle on page 10.

Read poems about the wind on page 4.

Find out how wind can light up your house on page 38.

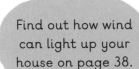

Discover how the wind helps birds to fly on page 46.

Wind and Nature

Windy World

Make your own kite on page 56.

Windy poems

Think about how the wind feels when it's blowing by. Can you write your own windy poem?

The wind blew

The wind was full of tricks today
It almost blew our cat away!
It chased a trash can down the street
And tried to blow me off my feet.
But next time that I go outside
The wind won't take me for a ride.
Because I know just what to do...
I'll cover both my shoes in glue!

I see the wind

I see the wind when the leaves dance by.
I see the wind when the clothes wave "Hi!"
I see the wind when the trees bend low.
I see the wind when the flags all blow.

I see the wind when the kites fly high.
I see the wind when the clouds race by.
I see the wind when it blows my hair.
I see the wind everywhere!

Why does the wind blow?

Air is so thin, light, and invisible,
it's easy to forget it's there.
But air is everywhere.

From a gentle breeze...

...to a STRONG gale...

...wind is simply air on the move.

Stormy winds

When air starts moving, it's hard to ignore.
Wind can whip up waves, or blow snow in a
blizzard. It can bring clouds and rain, or
warmer **weather**. It can lift kites, or topple
trees. It can stir up **storms**, or cool us down
on a hot day.

Warm air rises

Warm air is even lighter
and thinner than cooler air.
Think about the air trapped in a
hot air balloon. The burner makes
the air inside the balloon warmer and
lighter than the air around it. The
warmer air rises up, taking
the balloon along
for the ride!

Air is heated
by the Sun

Warmer air rises up, up, up

Cooler air rushes
in to fill the space
left behind.

What makes air move?

When the Sun warms the Earth's surface, the air next to
the surface gets warmer too. This warm air rises up, just
like the air in a hot air balloon. It leaves a space behind.
Cooler air from somewhere else rushes in to fill the
space. This moving air is wind.

Spinning snakes

You can't see warm air rising because air is invisible. But you can see what happens when it makes these snakes spin!

Toolkit

- Large piece of foil
- A piece of white printer paper or greaseproof paper
- Knitting needle or blunt pencil
- Scissors

What to do

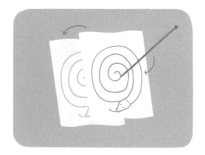

1 Trace the template on page 61. Place the printer paper on top of the foil, and draw over the lines with the knitting needle to transfer the pattern to the foil.

2 Cut out the circle. Then cut along the spiral line, from the outside of the circle to the center. Then open out the spiral.

3 Tape the knitting needle to a ledge or windowsill above a radiator, with the tip pointing up.

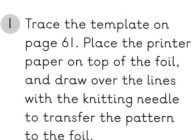

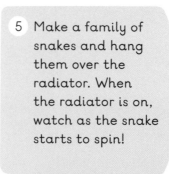

5 Make a family of snakes and hang them over the radiator. When the radiator is on, watch as the snake starts to spin!

4 Rest the very center of the foil circle on the tip of the knitting needle. Press gently to make a dent in the foil. The spiral should balance on the dent.

What happens?

It's not magic—it's air on the move! Air heated by the radiator rises up. Cooler air rushes in from other parts of the room to take the place of the rising warm air. This air is heated too, and rises to keep your snakes moving.

Never hang anything over a fire, electric heater, or flame. It could catch on fire.

The Wind Eagle

Thousands of years ago, no one knew why the wind blew. People in different parts of the world told stories about the wind. This Native American story, told by the Abenaki, imagines that a giant bird causes the wind.

Gluscabi lived with his grandmother by a big lake. One day, he got into his canoe and began to paddle across the water, but a strong wind turned his canoe around. Gluscabi tried again and again, but each time the wind blew him back to the shore.

Gluscabi stomped back home and asked his grandmother where the wind came from. "Far from here, on a tall mountain, stands a great eagle," she said. "When he flaps his wings, the wind blows."

Gluscabi walked for a long, long time, until he reached the mountain where the Wind Eagle sat. He tricked the Wind Eagle into letting him tie its wings together. Then he went back home.

When Gluscabi got back to the lake, there was no wind at all. The air was hot and still. The land was dry. The water was dirty. Gluscabi realized he had made a terrible mistake. "We need the wind," his grandmother said. "It keeps the air cool and clean, and brings the clouds that give us rain. It moves the water and keeps it fresh."

Can you write a story about the wind?

Gluscabi trekked all the way back to the place where he had left the Wind Eagle. He untied the great bird. "It's good that the wind blows," Gluscabi said, "but it's also good when the air is still sometimes." The Wind Eagle agreed, and to this day sometimes there is wind and sometimes it is still.

How strong is the wind?

Just over 200 years ago, a British sea captain called Francis Beaufort came up with a way to gauge the strength of the wind.

The **Beaufort scale** describes what the sea or trees look like when the wind is blowing at different speeds. You don't need any equipment to use the Beaufort scale—just your eyes.

The Beaufort Scale was used for the first time on the famous voyage of the *Beagle* (page 30).

0 CALM

Wind speed: Less than 1 mph

1 LIGHT AIR

Wind speed: 1–3 mph

2 LIGHT BREEZE

Wind speed: 4–7 mph

3 GENTLE BREEZE

Wind speed: 8–12 mph

4 MODERATE BREEZE

Wind speed: 13–18 mph

5 FRESH BREEZE

Wind speed: 19–24 mph

6 A STRONG BREEZE

Wind speed: 25–31 mph

7 NEAR GALE

Wind speed: 32–38 mph

8 GALE

Wind speed: 39–46 mph

9 STRONG GALE

Wind speed: 47–54 mph

10 STORM

Wind speed: 55–63 mph

11 VIOLENT STORM

Wind speed: 64–72 mph

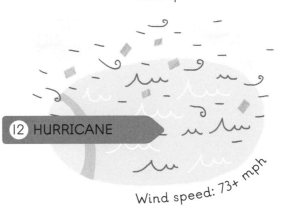

12 HURRICANE

Wind speed: 73+ mph

13

Measure wind speed

Make an **anemometer** to measure the speed of the wind.

Toolkit

- Four identical plastic bottles
- Five wooden skewers
- Plastic bead
- Push pin
- Scissors and tape
- Foam ball or cube
- Drinking straw
- Colorful paint

What to do

1 Use the skewer to poke a hole through the very center of the foam ball or cube.

2 Push the drinking straw through the hole and trim the ends.

3 Draw a line around each plastic bottle, exactly 4 inches from the top. Ask your grown-up to cut around the lines to make four plastic "cups". Paint each cup a bright color.

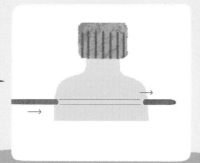

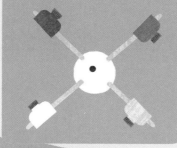

4 Use the push pin to poke holes in opposite sides of one cup. Push a skewer through the holes.

5 Push the other end of the skewer into the foam ball. Repeat steps 4 and 5 with the other three cups, joining one to each side of the ball.

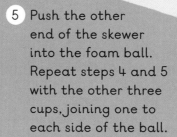

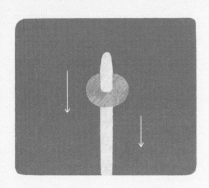

6 Find a plastic bead with a hole the same diameter as the remaining skewer. Push it onto one end of the skewer.

7 Slide the ball onto the skewer so that it rests on the bead. Make sure all the cups are level and facing in the same direction.

8 Tape the upright skewer to a heavy object (such as a bottle of water) or push it into a pot of soil or sand. Set up the anemometer in an open space, away from trees and buildings.

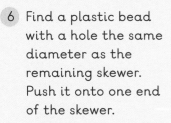

What happens?

When wind pushes on the cups, the anemometer will spin. The faster the wind is moving, the faster it spins. Watch one of the colored cups to count how many times the anemometer spins around in 15 seconds. Multiply this number by four to record the number of turns per minute.

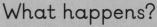

Using your anemometer, record how windy it is on different days. The more turns per minute, the windier it is!

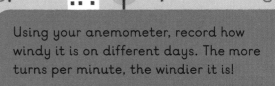

15

Follow the wind

Explore the windiest parts of the world, but don't get stuck in the **doldrums**!

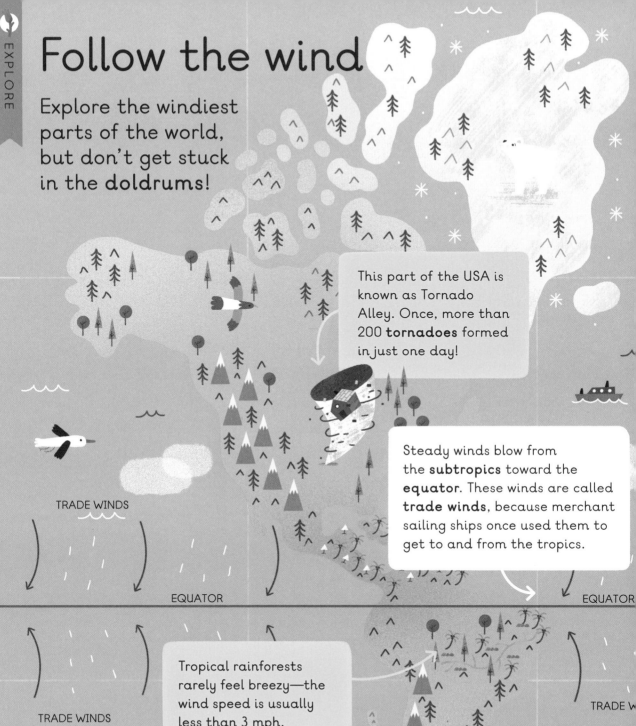

This part of the USA is known as Tornado Alley. Once, more than 200 **tornadoes** formed in just one day!

Steady winds blow from the **subtropics** toward the **equator**. These winds are called **trade winds**, because merchant sailing ships once used them to get to and from the tropics.

TRADE WINDS

EQUATOR

EQUATOR

Tropical rainforests rarely feel breezy—the wind speed is usually less than 3 mph.

TRADE WINDS

TRADE W

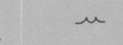

Antarctica is the windiest **continent**. Hurricane-strength winds can last for weeks or months.

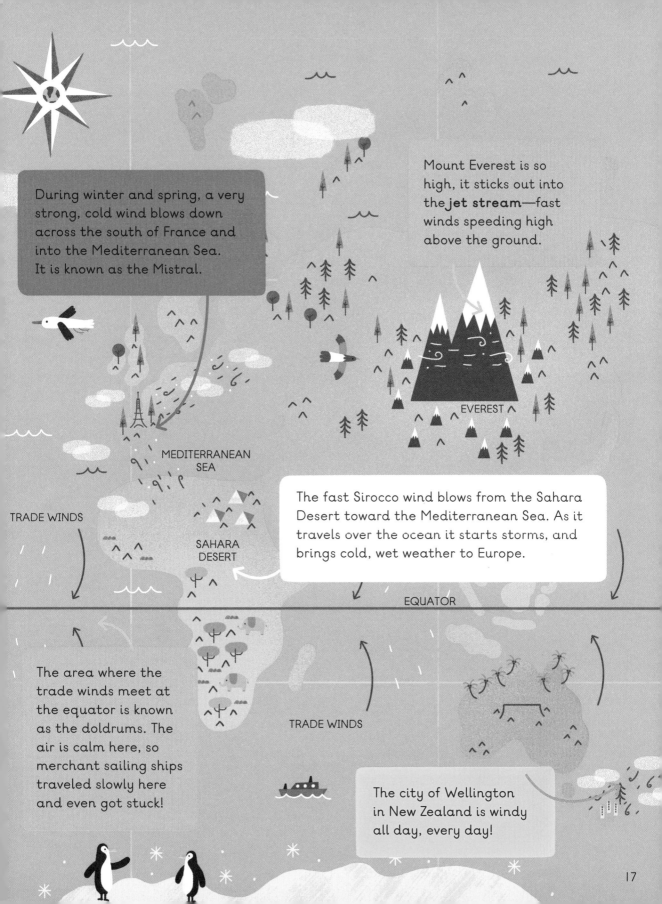

During winter and spring, a very strong, cold wind blows down across the south of France and into the Mediterranean Sea. It is known as the Mistral.

Mount Everest is so high, it sticks out into the **jet stream**—fast winds speeding high above the ground.

MEDITERRANEAN SEA

EVEREST

The fast Sirocco wind blows from the Sahara Desert toward the Mediterranean Sea. As it travels over the ocean it starts storms, and brings cold, wet weather to Europe.

TRADE WINDS

SAHARA DESERT

EQUATOR

The area where the trade winds meet at the equator is known as the doldrums. The air is calm here, so merchant sailing ships traveled slowly here and even got stuck!

TRADE WINDS

The city of Wellington in New Zealand is windy all day, every day!

17

Make a windsock

Windsocks dance and flutter in the wind. Recycle a plastic bag to make your own windsock.

Toolkit

- Thin plastic shopping bag
- Empty, clean yogurt or sour cream container (the larger the better)
- String or yarn
- Hole punch
- Tape
- Scissors
- Stick or dowel

What to do

1. Ask a grown-up to help you cut the rim off the plastic pot (about ½ to ¾ inches), to make a plastic ring.

2. Punch holes in four opposite sides of the plastic ring.

3. Cut the bottom off the plastic bag, and cut one side so it opens to make a large rectangle.

4. Wrap the plastic rectangle around the ring, and mark where it meets. Cut the plastic down to size, then tape it in place. Join the ends of the rectangle to form a tube.

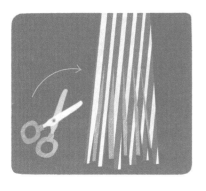
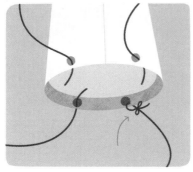

5 Cut the bottom half of the plastic tube into strips that will flutter in the wind.

6 Carefully poke through the plastic over the four holes you made earlier. Cut four pieces of string, 12 to 16 inches long. Loop a piece of string through each hole, and knot it in place.

7 Gather the four ends and knot them together. Tie them to the top of the stick.

Look out for large windsocks near airports.

They show pilots which way the wind is blowing.

Plastic is waterproof, so you can leave your windsock outside!

8 Attach the stick to a fencepost or another high place outside. Watch as the windsock catches the wind.

Predicting the weather

The Ancient Greeks imagined the wind as gods with separate personalities. This helped them to **predict** the weather brought by winds from the North, South, East, or West. The gods were said to have the power to make crops grow well, or destroy them with bad weather.

WEST: Zephyros

Wind from the West was gentle and brought warm weather in the spring. The Ancient Greeks imagined this god as a young man carrying flowers.

SOUTH: Notos

Wind from the South was hot and dry, causing storms. Notos is tipping out water, like rain.

W

S

NORTH: Boreas

The cold north wind brought wintery weather. The Greek god of the North Wind has warm clothes. He is blowing through a large shell, to make the howling noise of strong wind.

EAST: Euros

Euros was the god of the East wind, bringing rainy weather in summer and autumn. His cloak looks like heavy clouds.

Make a weather vane

A **weather vane** shows which direction the wind is blowing from. Make your own and use it to predict the weather.

Toolkit

- Thin cardboard, e.g. an old cereal box
- Knitting needle or long wooden skewer
- Pen lid
- Plastic bottle
- Two drinking straws
- Push pin
- Scissors, glue, and tape

What to do

1 Trace the template on page 61 and transfer it to the cardboard. Cut out two matching arrows.

2 Place the pen lid between the two arrows, and hold it in place with tape.

3 Lay one drinking straw over the other at right angles. Push the pin through both to make a small hole.

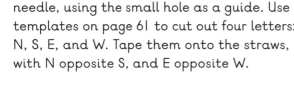

4 Carefully push the straws onto the knitting needle, using the small hole as a guide. Use the templates on page 61 to cut out four letters: N, S, E, and W. Tape them onto the straws, with N opposite S, and E opposite W.

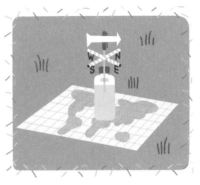

5 Tape the knitting needle to a bottle full of water, as shown.

6 Slide the pen lid onto the point of the knitting needle. Blow on the arrow to make sure that it spins around easily.

7 Put your weather vane in an open space, away from walls and trees. Use a compass or a map to help you point the N toward North.

Which way is the wind blowing?

What happens?

The arrow swings around in the wind until it is pointing toward the direction the wind is coming from. Use the Beaufort Scale (page 12), your anemometer (page 14), and your weather vane to keep a diary. Write down what the wind is like each morning, and what kind of weather you have that day. Do you notice any patterns?

Wind chill

Has a gust of wind ever made you sh-sh-shiver? It's because wind cools your skin, and makes the weather feel colder than it really is. This effect is known as **wind chill**.

The temperature outside is 32°F —perfect for playing in the snow.

The temperature outside is 32°F but the breeze makes it feel like 21°F.

Try this...

Dip one finger in water and hold your hand up in the wind. What do you see and feel? The wet finger starts to dry, and it starts to feel colder than the other fingers. The evaporating water is taking heat from your finger.

What happens?

Wet skin loses heat faster than dry skin. This is why your skin sweats to help you stay cool on a warm day. As the water in sweat evaporates (dries up) it takes heat from your skin. Wind makes water evaporate more quickly, cooling your skin even faster. This is why a breeze feels so nice on a warm day.

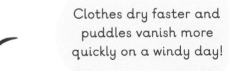

Clothes dry faster and puddles vanish more quickly on a windy day!

Testing windspeed

Investigate how wind speeds up **evaporation**. Dip your hands in water and make two wet handprints on a sheet of paper. Cut the paper in half and put one handprint outside in a sheltered place, and one in a windy place (use stones to weigh the paper down). Which handprint disappears first?

Inside a storm

Some winds are much faster and stronger than others. The strongest, most powerful winds happen during storms. Tornadoes are the wildest windstorms in the world.

Tornadoes are made of super-fast winds that reach down from storms in a funnel shape. They form when cold air meets warm air and starts to spiral. Some tornadoes are so powerful that they can lift roofs, cars, or trucks off the ground.

The world's fastest winds happened inside tornadoes. They have reached 300 miles per hour, which is the same speed as the fastest trains.

The widest tornado was 1 mile across —that's 160 buses hood to bumper!

Wild weather

Wild weather has inspired many stories. *The Wizard of Oz* is a famous story that begins when a tornado picks up a house and drops it in a strange and magical land!

Tornado in a bottle

What to do

Toolkit

- Clear plastic bottle with a screw lid
- Water
- Grown-up helper
- Mounting putty or masking tape

1. Ask your grown-up to poke two small holes— one near the base of the bottle, and one in the center of the lid.

2. Put a piece of mounting putty over the hole at the base of the bottle. Then fill the bottle with water and put the lid on.

A "tornado" forms as the water drains out of the bottle!

3. With your thumb over the hole in the lid, turn the bottle upside down. Carefully peel off the tape.

4. Move the bottle around quickly in a circular motion to get the water swirling. Now take your thumb off the hole at the bottom.

Harnessing the wind

Think about the strongest
wind you have ever felt.

Perhaps a gust of wind whipped
a kite or umbrella out of your hands.

Perhaps you had to lean into
wind that pushed you backward.

Perhaps you dropped some paper
and watched the wind whisk it away.

Wind energy

Whenever the wind pushes an object
along or lifts it into the air, the wind's
energy is doing work. Wouldn't it be
great if we could harness this energy
and make it do useful work for us?
For thousands of years, people found
ways to do just that.

Plain sailing

The first boats were wooden rafts and canoes that had to be paddled from place to place. People **power** was tiring and not very speedy (have you ever seen a quick getaway in a rowboat?). No wonder people began using the wind to give them a push!

A strong mast joins a sail to a boat, so the whole boat moves when the wind pushes the sail. The energy in the moving wind is transferred to the boat.

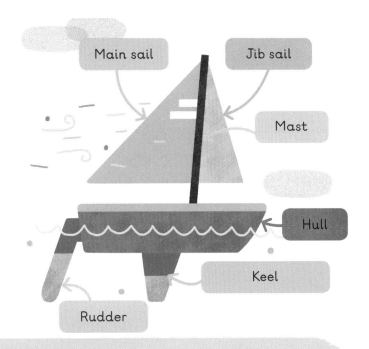

Main sail

Jib sail

Mast

Hull

Keel

Rudder

Try this...

Cut two identical "rafts" from corrugated cardboard. Fold a piece of thin cardboard at right angles and stick it to one of the rafts. Float both rafts in a bathtub full of water. What happens when you blow on them?

What happens?

The wind pushes both rafts along, but the raft with the sail moves farther and faster. Adding a sail means that the moving air has a much bigger area to push on.

Find out more about sails by making a wind-powered racer on page 32–33.

Ships ahoy!

Wind changed the world by pushing boats here, there, and everywhere.

500 years ago, explorers such as Christopher Columbus used sailing ships to set up links between Europe and the Americas.

In the 1800s, Charles Darwin sailed the world in the HMS *Beagle*. The things he saw helped him to come up with his famous theory of evolution by natural selection.

400 years ago, Spanish galleons delivered people and goods to the Americas, and returned laden with treasure.

150 years ago, sails were helping fishing boats to travel faster and farther.

1200 years ago, Vikings used longships to carry out daring raids.

1800 years ago, the Ancient Romans used sailing ships to carry goods and people around their enormous empire.

200 years ago, long before tanks or airplanes were invented, warships such as HMS *Victory* fought battles at sea.

5000 years ago, sails helped the Egyptians carry people and goods up and down the Nile.

2000 years ago, Chinese junks helped China trade with Africa and Asia.

150 years ago, fast sailing ships such as the *Cutty Sark* carried goods around the world.

240 years ago, sailing ships carried Europeans to settle in Australia.

Sail racers

Make wind-powered
vehicles to race on land.

Toolkit

- Letter-size piece of thin cardstock
- Drinking straw
- 4 cotton swabs
- 6 small toy wheels
- Ruler
- Scissors
- Tape

What to do

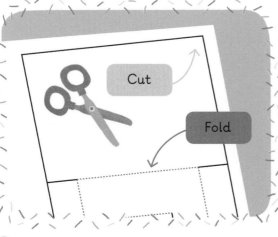

1. Trace or copy the template on page 60 onto the cardstock. Cut along the solid lines. Fold along the dashed lines.

2. Cut the drinking straw into three pieces as shown. Turn the cardstock over and tape the straw pieces to the bottom of the card.

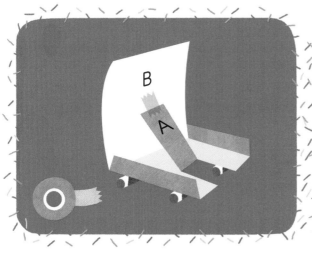

3. Turn the card over and fold along the dotted lines. Tape A to B to make a sail.

4. Push one cotton swab through the long straw. Push a toy wheel onto each cotton tip.

5 Cut the second cotton swab in half. Push the cut ends into the short pieces of drinking straw. Push a toy wheel onto the cotton tips.

6 Make a second sail racer by following steps 1 to 5.

Racing

Now all you need is wind. You could pick a windy day and race outside (try to pick a smooth surface to race on). You can also create your own "wind" by flapping a magazine or blowing just behind the sail, or use an electric fan (don't forget to ask an adult first).

On your marks, get set...blow!

The wind pushes against the sail.

The sail is attached to the vehicle, so the whole thing is pushed forward.

Can you design a better sail racer?

Try this...

• What happens if you make the sail racer heavier? (Try sliding paper clips onto the base, or sticking on lumps of modeling clay.)

• What happens if you make the sail bigger? (Try sticking sheets of paper of different sizes over the sail.)
• Does it make a difference if you make the sail wider or taller?

Windmills

Sails can also be used to harness wind energy on land. A windmill's sails are joined to a **shaft**. When the sails are pushed by the wind, the shaft turns around and around.

Anything joined to the shaft will turn around and around too. This might be a millstone, to grind grain, a pump to move water from place to place, or a circular saw to cut wood.

The sails are pushed by the wind.

A windmill is a giant machine that uses wind to get other objects moving.

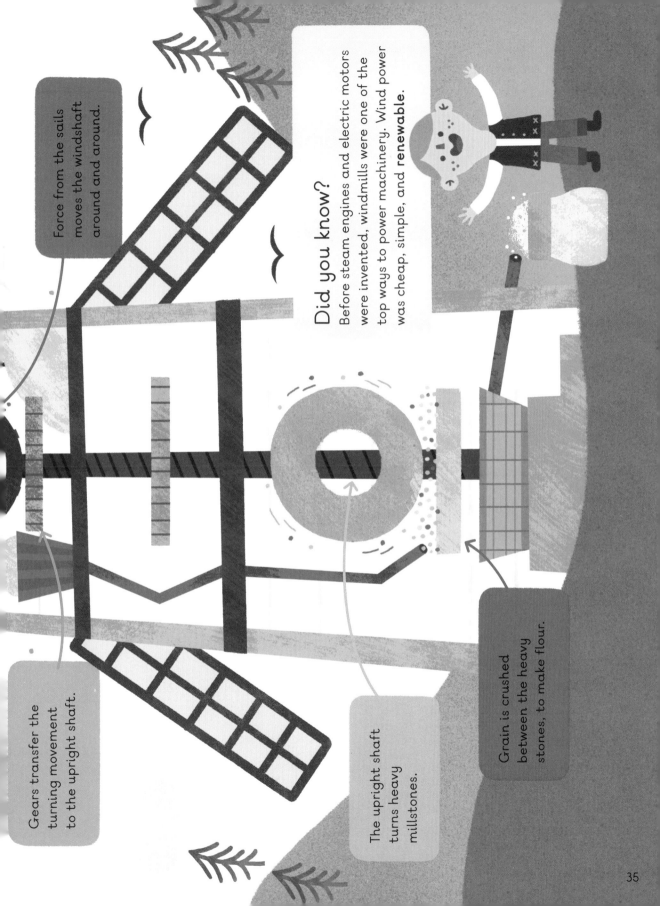

Force from the sails moves the windshaft around and around.

Did you know?

Before steam engines and electric motors were invented, windmills were one of the top ways to power machinery. Wind power was cheap, simple, and **renewable**.

Gears transfer the turning movement to the upright shaft.

The upright shaft turns heavy millstones.

Grain is crushed between the heavy stones, to make flour.

Make a pinwheel

Make a pinwheel and harness the wind's energy to lift a paper clip. Does the direction the wind is blowing in make a difference?

Toolkit

- Plastic bottle of water
- Wooden toothpick
- Three beads that fit tightly on the toothpick
- Drinking straw
- 6 x 6 inch square of stiff paper
- Scissors, ruler, and tape
- Paper clip and thread

What to do

1 Fold the paper along each diagonal. Cut along each fold line from the corners, stopping about ¾ inch before you reach the center of the square.

2 Fold alternate points into the center. Resting on cardboard, push the toothpick through all five layers of paper.

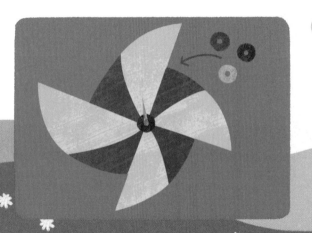

3 Use two beads to hold the paper in place on either side.

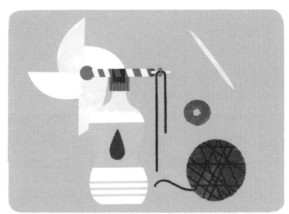

4 Cut a piece of drinking straw about ¾ inch shorter than the toothpick. Tape it onto the lid of the bottle.

5 Then feed the free end of the toothpick through the straw. Push the end of the thread through a bead, then push the bead onto the toothpick to hold the thread firmly in place. Blow on your pinwheel to make sure that it spins.

6 Tie a small paper clip to the end of the thread. Then blow on the pinwheel to wind up the thread, and lift the paper clip up.

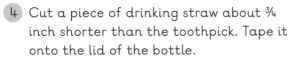

Try this...

Challenge your friends—who can lift a paper clip the greatest distance with a single breath? One, two, three—blow!

From wind to wire

Just like the windmill uses power from the wind to grind grain, a wind turbine can change energy from the wind into electricity. We can use electricity to power millions of useful things, from machines and lights, to cars and computers.

What happens?

As the Sun warms the Earth's land and water, air near the surface is warmed up too. It is the Sun's energy that causes wind (see pages 6-7).

The moving wind has lots of energy. It pushes on the turbine blades. The blades turn.

Electricity is a type of energy that can travel through wires, to the places it is needed. You don't have to live near a wind turbine to use energy from the wind!

Now the blades have lots of energy. They turn a shaft, which turns a **generator**. The generator makes electricity.

Blade

Shaft

Generator

Tower

How have you used electricity today?

Each turbine can make enough electricity for more than 1000 homes.

Making music

Make a pretty wind chime and enjoy music made by the wind on a breezy day.

Toolkit

- Old cardboard tube
- Pen or pencil, scissors and a ruler
- Yarn or string
- Tape
- Small, light metal objects such as old jar lids, spare screws, and old keys
- Bright paint and paper

What to do

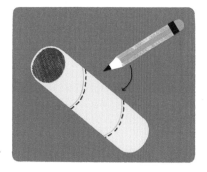

1 Draw a spiral on the tube from top to bottom. Most cardboard tubes have a line that you can follow.

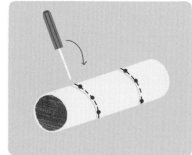

2 Make dots about every 1 inch along the line. Ask an adult to punch a hole in each dot.

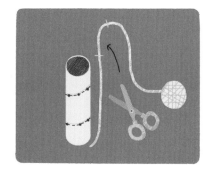

3 Cut a piece of yarn or string 2 inches longer than the tube. Tie a knot at one end.

4 Push the other end through one of the holes, toward the center of the tube. Reach up inside the tube and pull the yarn to the bottom.

5 Tie one of your metal objects to the string.

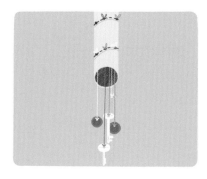

6 Repeat steps 4, 5, and 6 for each of the other holes.

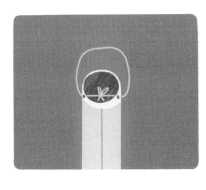

7 Use tape to join the ends of the yarn to the tube. Wrap the tube in colorful paper to hide the ends.

8 Ask your grown-up to poke two holes on opposite sides of the top of the tube. Thread a piece of yarn through the holes and tie a knot to make a handle.

Metal objects are good for making wind chimes because they make a chiming or ringing noise when they bang into each other. Choose objects of different sizes to play different notes!

Decorate the tube, and paint the metal objects, to make your wind chime look as good as it sounds! Hang your wind chime next to a window, or on a covered porch.

41

Carried on the wind

Each seed made by a plant can grow into a brand new plant. Plants need to spread their seeds as far as possible, so that they don't all start growing in the same place. Some plants use the wind to help spread their seeds.

We all need our own space, water, and sunlight!

Which of these seeds do you think are spread by the wind?

They are ALL spread by the wind, in different ways!

Seeds with wings

Some tree seeds have wings to fly or **glide**. The wings make the seeds spin as they fall to the ground. This slows them down, so they travel farther from the tree.

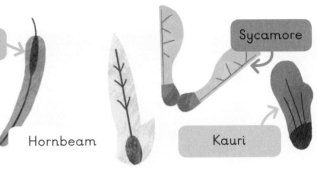

Ash

Sycamore

Hornbeam

Kauri

Drifting seeds

Some seeds have fluffy parachutes to help them drift through the air.

Bulrush

Swan

Liatrus

Thistle

Blow on a dandelion and watch the tiny seeds float away...

Pods that are shaken

Some seeds grow in pods that are shaken by the wind. The seeds fall out of the pod and away from the plant.

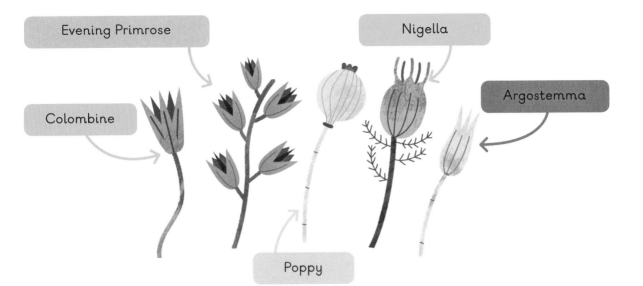

Evening Primrose

Nigella

Colombine

Argostemma

Poppy

Seed spinners

Engineers have studied spinning seeds to help them design aircraft! Experiment with seed spinners to design your own super spinner.

Toolkit

- Letter-size paper
- Pencil, ruler, and scissors
- Mounting putty or modeling clay

What to do

① Draw a straight line across the paper, a little over 1 inch from the bottom.

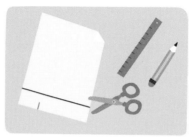

② Cut out the strip. Find the center of the strip. Make a pencil mark 1¼ inch to the left of this. Draw a line from the bottom to the top of the strip, stopping halfway.

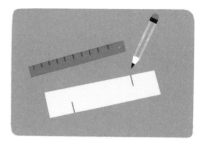

③ Make a pencil mark 1¼ inch to the right of the center. This time, draw a line from the top to the bottom of the strip, stopping halfway.

④ Cut along the lines.

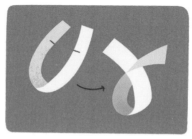

⑤ Bend and twist the strip, to push the cut paper together. You have created the two wings of your spinner.

⑥ Stick a small ball of mounting putty at the base of the loop. This is the seed.

7 Make more spinners. Try making the wings longer or shorter by making the pencil marks closer or farther from the center of the strip.

Try this...

Try making better spinners. You could try different types of paper, different shaped wings, or heavier seeds. Which spinner stays in the air for the longest?

8 Ask an adult to help you to find a safe place to drop the seed spinner from a height. Watch it spin as it falls to the floor.

Seeds with two wings are often called "helicopter seeds". They twirl like a helicopter before falling to the ground.

What happens?

Some tree seeds spin like this as they fall to the ground. This keeps them in the air for longer, making it more likely that a gust of wind will blow them away from the tree.

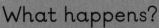

Away with the wind

Animals also use the wind in different ways.

> We can travel for hundreds of miles!

Large birds of prey such as condors use the wind to travel hundreds of miles without flapping their wings. This saves energy.

Many butterflies and moths fly to warmer places for the winter. They fly high up into the air and hitch a ride on fast-moving winds to travel as fast as a car on a highway!

Condor

By soaring on the wind, some vultures can fly as high as a jumbo jet!

Albatross

Albatrosses have the world's longest wings. They are experts at swooping and soaring. By catching the wind in their wings and sailing upward, an albatross can fly for days without flapping its wings.

Vulture

Sometimes the wind picks up unexpected passengers. Frogs and fishes have rained down from the sky after being swept up by a tornado.

Some spiderlings (baby spiders) are carried by the wind to a new home. They climb to the tip of a twig or blade of grass and spin a tiny thread of silk, which catches the wind like a parachute.

Assassin bugs use the wind to help them hunt spiders. They wait for a gust of wind to shake the spider's web, so the spider doesn't feel them coming.

Assassin bug

Make a wind trap

Find out what the wind is carrying through your garden.

Toolkit

- Lids from plastic tubs
- Plastic wrap
- Petroleum jelly (Vaseline®)
- Wooden skewers
- White cardboard
- Magnifying glass or microscope

What to do

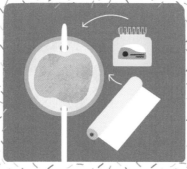

1. Poke two holes on opposite sides of a plastic lid. Push the skewer through the holes.

2. Place the plastic wrap tightly around the lid. Carefully smear the plastic wrap with petroleum jelly.

3. Follow steps 1 and 2 to make more wind traps.

4. Set your wind traps up outside, by pushing the end of the skewer into a pot of soil or sand. Try placing traps at different distances from the ground. Leave the traps outside for two or three days.

5 Bring them inside and take the plastic wrap off, keeping the sticky surface up. Wrap it around a piece of white cardboard. Use a magnifying glass or microscope to look at what you've collected.

It may look like dust—but look closer. Can you spot any of these?

Grains of sand

Strong winds can spread sand from the world's deserts for thousands of miles. Grains of sand in your garden may have once been part of a sand **dune** in the Sahara!

Tree pollen

The pollen of many trees is carried on the wind. It can cause hay fever. Some types of pollen look spiky under a microscope.

Space rocks

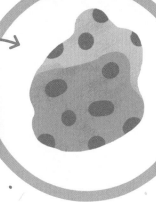

Thousands of tiny space rocks fall to Earth's surface every day. These micrometeorites are small enough to be carried on the wind. You can spot them because they are magnetic.

Wild wind

There are lots of ways to use the wind to have fun! Have you tried any of these?

Hot air balloon

Hot air balloons rise up because they are filled with warm air, but they need wind to move them from place to place.

Boat sailing

Today, most boats to transport people or cargo have engines but sailing boats are still popular for sport.

Racing yacht

Sailboats used for sport can be small dinghies for one person, or huge racing yachts, which need a crew of 10 sailors.

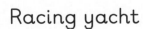

Kiteboarding

Kiteboarders use the wind to pull their surfboard along. They can do jumps and tricks.

Kite buggy

A large kite can harness the wind to pull vehicles on land. Smooth, flat sand is perfect for going fast! On snow, kites can be used to pull snowboards and sleds.

Windsurfing

Windsurfers stand on a board attached to a sail that is pushed along by the wind.

Gliding

Launch this paper glider into the air and see how far it flies. Can you hitch a lift on the wind like a real glider?

Toolkit

- Thick letter-size paper
- Ruler, pencil, scissors
- Tape
- Small coin

What to do

1 Draw a line from top to bottom of the paper, about 1¼ inch from the edge.

2 Fold the paper along the line. Cut along the line marked by the edge.

3 Cut the strip of folded paper in half.

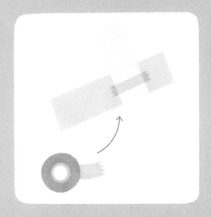

4 Join the pieces with tape to make the body and wings of your glider.

5 Cut the wings into a curved shape.

6 Cut another 1¼ inch strip of paper, and cut it in half. Fold one piece in half.

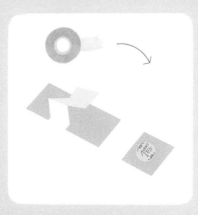

7   Fold the top flap back to the crease. Turn the paper over and repeat on the other side.

8   This zigzag of paper will be the tail of your glider. Use tape to join it to the back of the glider.

9   Tape a small coin to the nose of the glider. You can hide this inside the fold if you like.

Launch your glider by holding the body between your fingertips, and moving your arm forward quickly.

Did you know?

Like your paper planes, real gliders don't have engines. They can stay up in the sky for a long time by hitching a lift on the wind. Jet planes do not need wind to fly—but they do need air. Hot gases shoot out of the back of a jet engine. This pushes the plane forward through the air. Air rushes over the wings and produces a force called lift, which moves the plane up into the sky.

Let's go fly a kite!

Can you match each kite to its owner?

Experiments with kites helped the Wright Brothers to design the world's first working aircraft!

Kites must be light but strong.

Fly kites in wide, open spaces, and never near power lines. Electricity could travel down the line.

A kite's tail is not just for decoration. It makes sure the nose stays up, which keeps the kite stable.

Kites were first used more than 2000 years ago, in China.

In 2014, a kite flown in Australia soared to nearly 16,000 feet—the height of Europe's tallest mountain, Mont Blanc!

In 2011, children of the Gaza Strip set a world record 12,530 by flying the kites at the same time.

Stunt kites have two or four lines. They can perform tricks, such as flying in a figure eight.

Make a kite

Kites must be light but strong. This paper kite is perfect for flying on a breezy day.

Toolkit

- Rectangle of scrap paper, e.g. a page from an old magazine or comic book
- Spool of thread or fine string
- Tape
- Drinking straw
- Hole punch

What to do

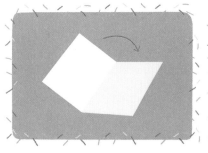

1 Fold the paper in half so the short ends meet.

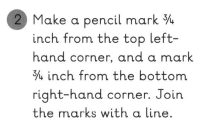

2 Make a pencil mark ¾ inch from the top left-hand corner, and a mark ¾ inch from the bottom right-hand corner. Join the marks with a line.

3 Fold the paper along this line, and unfold.

4 Turn the paper over. Fold the top flap back, following the crease. You will be able to see a rough diamond shape.

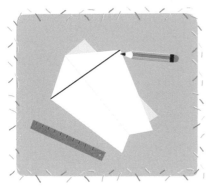

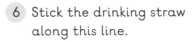

5 Draw a line across the diamond, from corner to corner.

6 Stick the drinking straw along this line.

7 Turn the paper over. Tape a long strip of plastic or paper to the bottom of the diamond to make the kite's tail.

8 Stick a piece of tape over the "spine" of the kite, about a quarter of the way from the top. Use a hole punch to make a hole through the paper. The tape will stop the paper from tearing as you fly the kite.

9 Use the hole to join the end of the thread to the kite. Then get ready to fly your kite!

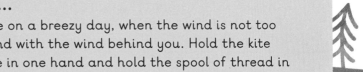

Try this...

Test the kite on a breezy day, when the wind is not too strong. Stand with the wind behind you. Hold the kite by the spine in one hand and hold the spool of thread in the other. When the kite catches the wind, let out a little thread at a time so the kite can move higher and higher.

Out of this world

Earth is not the only planet with windy weather. Get ready for a whirlwind tour of our solar system.

Mars
Winds on Mars are slower than on Earth, but they can whip up dust storms that last for weeks.

Venus
The temperature on Venus is similar everywhere on the planet, so winds blow more slowly than on Earth.

Mercury
Mercury has a very thin atmosphere, so there is no wind at all.

Earth
Most of the planets have an atmosphere, but their "air" is made up of different gases than the air on Earth.

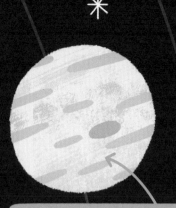

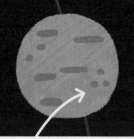

Neptune
Neptune has the fastest winds in the solar system. They race around the planet at up to 1500 miles per hour.

Jupiter
Jupiter's Great Red Spot is a hurricane so big it can be seen from Earth. The storm whizzes around Jupiter once every six days.

Titan
Winds on Saturn's moon Titan are strong enough to blow sand into huge dunes.

Saturn
Saturn's stripes are bands of cloud, blown around the planet by strong winds up to 1120 miles per hour.

Uranus
Icy cold winds on Uranus blow clouds along at more than 370 miles per hour.

In the vast empty space between planets there is no wind at all, because there is no air!

Templates

B

A

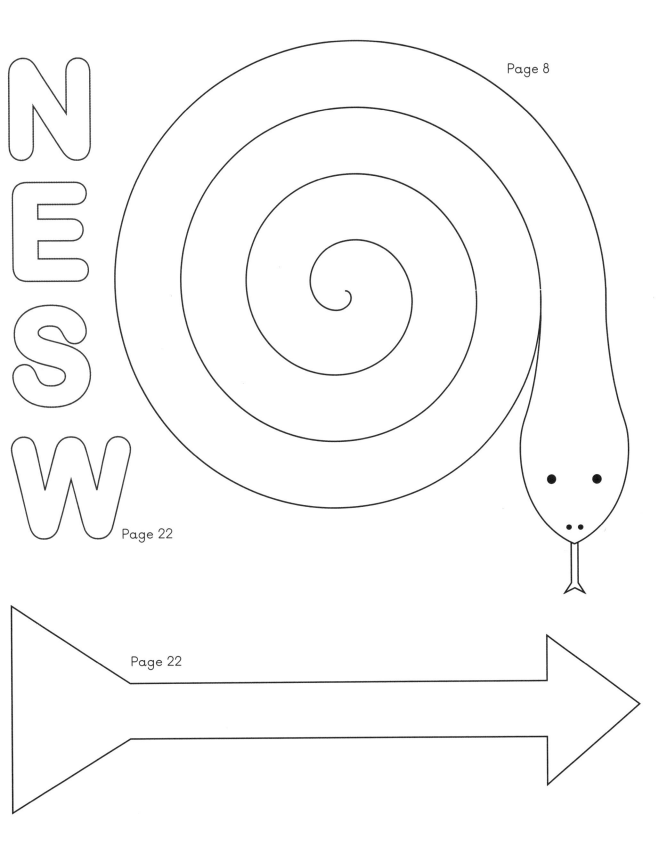

Page 8

Page 22

Page 22

Glossary

Anemometer A gadget for measuring the speed of the wind.

Atmosphere A thin layer of gases that surrounds the Earth and other planets.

Beaufort scale A way of describing how fast the wind is moving by looking at the effect it has on the sea or objects on land.

Blizzard A windy snowstorm, which makes it hard to see very far.

Continent One of the world's large areas of land.

Doldrums An area near the equator, where the sea is very calm.

Dune A mound formed by wind blowing sand into a mound.

Electricity A form of energy that can travel from place to place through wires.

Equator An imaginary line that divides the Earth into two halves (called hemispheres).

Evaporation When something turns from a liquid into a gas or vapor.

Gale A very strong wind.

Generator A machine that changes movement energy into electricity.

Glide To fly with no engine power.

Hurricane A storm with very fast winds.

Jet stream Very strong winds found 6-10 miles above the surface of the Earth.

Power Energy that is being used to do something.

Predict Figure out what will happen in the future.

Renewable It can be used over and over again without running out.

Shaft A long pole inside a machine that turns around and around. It is used to transfer power from one part of a machine to another.

Storm Bad weather with strong winds and rain, snow or hail, and sometimes thunder and lightning.

Sub-tropics The areas of the world a little farther North or South than the tropics.

Tornado A funnel of swirling winds that moves from place to place.

Trade winds Winds that blow steadily toward the equator.

Turbine A machine that can make electricity by using wind, water, steam, or gas to turn a special wheel that is connected to a generator.

Weather How hot, cold, cloudy, dry, or sunny a place is at a particular time.

Weather vane A device that spins around to show the direction the wind is coming from.

Wind chill The temperature that we feel, instead of the actual air temperature. The wind can make the temperature feel colder than it really is.

Index

Quarto is the authority on a wide range of topics.

Quarto educates, entertains and enriches the lives of our readers—enthusiasts and lovers of hands-on living.

www.quartoknows.com

Editor: Sophie Hallam
Designer: Clare Barber
Designed by: Mike Henson

Copyright © QEB Publishing 2016

First published in the United States in 2016 by QEB Publishing, Inc.
6 Orchard
Lake Forest, CA 92630

A CIP record for this book is available from the Library of Congress.

ISBN 978 1 68297 018 8

Printed in China